SUPREME

KENNY ABDO

Fly!
An Imprint of Abdo Zoom
abdobooks.com

abdobooks.com

Published by Abdo Zoom, a division of ABDO, P.O. Box 398166, Minneapolis,
Minnesota 55439. Copyright © 2023 by Abdo Consulting Group, Inc. International
copyrights reserved in all countries. No part of this book may be reproduced in any
form without written permission from the publisher. Fly!™ is a trademark and logo
of Abdo Zoom.

Printed in the United States of America, North Mankato, Minnesota.
052022
092022

THIS BOOK CONTAINS
RECYCLED MATERIALS

Photo Credits: Alamy, Getty Images, Shutterstock, Unsplash,
©Eden, Janine and Jim p.15/ CC BY 2.0
Production Contributors: Kenny Abdo, Jennie Forsberg, Grace Hansen
Design Contributors: Candice Keimig, Neil Klinepier, Laura Graphenteen

Library of Congress Control Number: 2021950288

Publisher's Cataloging-in-Publication Data

Names: Abdo, Kenny, author.
Title: Supreme / by Kenny Abdo.
Description: Minneapolis, Minnesota : Abdo Zoom, 2023 | Series: Hype brands |
    Includes online resources and index.
Identifiers: ISBN 9781098228576 (lib. bdg.) | ISBN 9781644948002 (pbk.) |
    ISBN 9781098229412 (ebook) | ISBN 9781098229832 (Read-to-Me ebook)
Subjects: LCSH: Clothing and dress--Juvenile literature. | Brand name products-
    Juvenile literature. | Supreme (Firm)--Juvenile literature. | Fashion--Social
    aspects--Juvenile literature. | Jebbia, James, 1963- --Juvenile literature. |
    Popularculture--Juvenile literature.
Classification: DDC 338.7--dc23

TABLE OF CONTENTS

SUPREME

Combining hip-hop, punk rock, and skateboarding culture, Supreme has created the ultimate streetwear hype.

The brand is known for its instant sellouts and super-limited **collaborations**. Fans wait in lines around the block ready to get their hands on the items as if they were works of art.

HYPE

James Jebbia worked at Stüssy's New York **flagship** in the early '90s. In 1994, he went into business for himself opening his first store in New York.

Selling mostly skateboards,
Jebbia's store also sold t-shirts
and sweats. He named his
passion project Supreme.

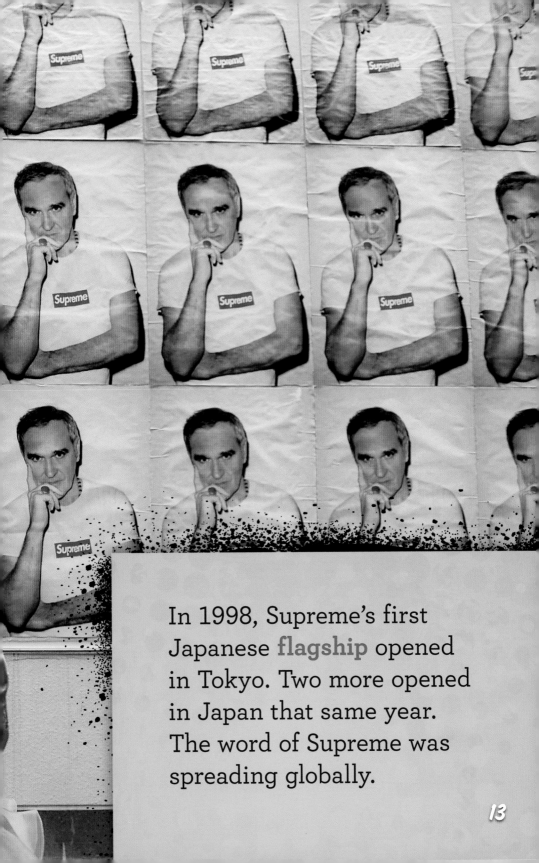

In 1998, Supreme's first Japanese **flagship** opened in Tokyo. Two more opened in Japan that same year. The word of Supreme was spreading globally.

13

ALL THE RAGE

Jebbia wanted nothing he released to be considered "limited." Instead, he wanted them to have short runs. In 2004, a second US location was opened in Los Angeles.

The Supreme online store opened in 2007. It offered fans around the world a chance to feel the hype. In 2008, Supreme notably **collaborated** with the famed New York City graffiti artist JA One.

Supreme releases two collections each year. The brand's **strategy** is to **drop** a few pieces from those collections online and in-store every Thursday.

Jebbia was interested in bringing
novelties to the world of fashion.
Supreme has come up with tons of
collectibles. From fire extinguishers to
limited edition Oreos.

In 2017, Supreme teamed up with fashion icon Louis Vuitton. It was one of the biggest **collaborations** of the year. In 2018, a collection of every Supreme **deck** was sold for $800,000 at **auction**!

Supreme **collaborated** with Japanese artist Takashi Murakami in 2020. Together, they raised $1 million for COVID-19 relief. They were able to take their hype and help people with it.

Going from a small skateboard shop to a billion-dollar titan, this fashion brand will always reign supreme.

GLOSSARY

auction – a sale at which goods are sold to the highest bidder.

collaborate – to work with another person or group in order to do something or reach a goal.

deck – the flat board that you stand on while skateboarding.

drop – when something that is highly anticipated is released to the public.

flagship – a brand's lead, largest, or most important store.

novelty – a product that is amusing because of its new or unusual quality.

strategy – a careful plan or method.

streetwear – fashionable, yet casual clothing worn by followers of popular culture. It is heavily influenced by hip-hop and surf culture.

ONLINE RESOURCES

Booklinks
NONFICTION NETWORK
FREE! ONLINE NONFICTION RESOURCES

To learn more about Supreme, please visit abdobooklinks.com or scan this QR code. These links are routinely monitored and updated to provide the most current information available.

INDEX